Antarctica

by Rebecca Hirsch

Content Consultant
Dr. John Cottle, Department of Earth Science
University of California, Santa Barbara

Reading Consultant
Jeanne Clidas
Reading Specialist

Children's Press®
An Imprint of Scholastic Inc.
New York • Toronto • London • Auckland • Sydney • Mexico City
New Delhi • Hong Kong • Danbury, Connecticut

Library of Congress Cataloging-in-Publication Data
Hirsch, Rebecca E.
  Antarctica / by Rebecca Hirsch ; content consultant, John Cottle.
      p. cm. – (Rookie read-about geography)
  Includes index.
  ISBN 978-0-531-28976-1 (lib.bdg.) – ISBN 978-0-531-29276-1 (pbk.)
  1. Antarctica–Juvenile literature. 2. Antarctica–Geography–Juvenile
literature. I. Cottle, John. II. Title.

  G863.H57 2013
  919.89–dc23

                              2012013398

1 2 3 4 5 6 7 8 9 10 R 22 21 20 19 18 17 16 15 14 13

Photographs © 2013: Alamy Images/David Tipling: 30; AP Images/Felicity
Aston: 12; Getty Images/Keren Su: 26; International Polar Foundation/
René Robert: 29; iStockphoto/Dean Bertoncelj: 14, 31 bottom left;
National Geographic Stock: cover (Sisse Brimberg & Cotton Coulson,
Keenpress), 18 (John Goodge), 20 (Kelly Jacques), 8, 31 bottom right
(Nick Powell); Photo Researchers/David Vaughan: 24; Shutterstock,
Inc./Gentoo Multimedia Ltd.: 4; Superstock, Inc.: 10, 31 top left (age
fotostock), 16, 31 top right (Minden Pictures), 22 (National Geographic).

Map by Matt Kania/www.maphero.com

Table of Contents

An Emperor penguin in Antarctica

Welcome to Antarctica!

Antarctica is an icy continent. It has no countries.

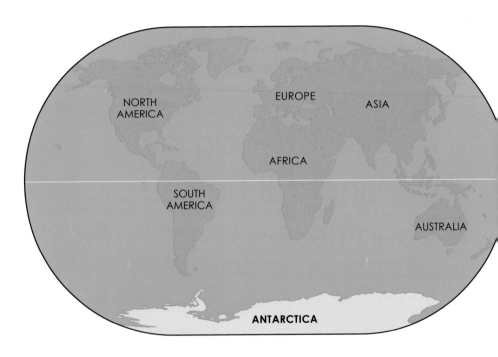

NORTH
AMERICA

EUROPE

ASIA

AFRICA

SOUTH
AMERICA

AUSTRALIA

ANTARCTICA

The largest pieces
of land on Earth are
continents. There are
seven. Antarctica is
the yellow continent
on this map.

Planes bring food and supplies to Antarctica.

People of Antarctica

Few people live in Antarctica. Most are scientists who come to study the continent.

Crabeater seals rest on the ice.

Visitors also come to watch seals and other amazing animals.

12

Felicity Aston skied across Antarctica
in 59 days.

Adventurers ski in Antarctica. Some ski to the South Pole. It is one of the coldest places on Earth.

Rockhopper penguins can hop
from rock to rock.

Amazing Animals

Antarctica is famous for its penguins. Rockhoppers live by the rocky shore.

A killer whale can swim very fast.

Killer whales swim in the icy water. They hunt for fish to eat.

Two scientists work in the Transantarctic Mountains.

Ice, Wind, and Snow

Antarctica has fierce winds that blow the snow. People must wear bright coats to see each other.

Mountains of the Antarctic Peninsula

Antarctica has tall mountains. Most are covered by ice and snow.

An iceberg in the Weddell Sea

Antarctica has thick sheets of ice. Giant ice chunks can break off into the ocean. These chunks are called icebergs.

Scientists measure floating sea ice.

Learning from Antarctica

Scientists come to Antarctica from many countries. They study the ice to learn about climate changes.

Scientists study a group of Emperor penguins.

Scientists study the animals and weather, too. There is so much to learn from Antarctica. Countries will always work together to protect this icy continent.

Modern Marvels

- Scientists in Antarctica work at Princess Elisabeth Station.

- The stainless steel walls have many layers to keep heat in and to keep cold winds out.

- Windmills on tall poles catch the wind to make electricity for the station.

Try It!

Why do the walls have many layers?
What do the windmills do?
If you made a building to keep cold winds out, what would it look like?

Meet a Wandering Albatross

- Wandering albatrosses lay their eggs on islands around Antarctica.

  - The male and female work together to raise their young.

  - They have the longest wingspan of any bird.

    - They fly far looking for squid and fish to eat.

Words You Know

iceberg

killer whale

penguin

plane

Index

Facts for Now

Visit this Scholastic Web site for more information on Antarctica:
www.factsfornow.scholastic.com
Enter the keyword **Antarctica**

About the Author

Rebecca Hirsch is a scientist-turned-writer and the author of many books for young readers.